Traditional Italian Recipes

1

Liquid Measures Conversion Chart

Fluid Ounces	U.S. Measures	Milliliters
	1 tps	5
1/4	2 tps	7
1/2	1 tbs	15
1	2 tbs	23
2	¼ cup	56
6	¾ cup	170
8	1 cup or ½ pint	225
9		250 – ¼ liter
18	2 ½ cups	500 – ½ liter
36	4 ½ cups	1000 - 1 liter
72	9 cups	2000 – 2 liter

Solid Measures Conversion Chart

Ounces	Pounds	Grams	Kilos
1		28	
3 ½		100	
4	1/4	112	
5		140	
8	1/2	225	
9		250	¼
12	3/4	340	
16	1	450	
18		500	½
20	1 ¼	560	
24	1 ½	675	
27		750	¾
28	1 ¾	780	
32	2	900	
36	2 ¼	1000	1

All conversions are approximate.
They have been rounded off to the nearest convenient measure

Traditional recipes of lucchesian farmers

maria pacini fazzi editore

© copyright: 1999, maria pacini fazzi editore
piazza s. romano, 16
55100 lucca
tel. 0583/55530 - fax 0583/418245
e-mail: mpf@pacinifazzi.it
sito in internet:
www.pacinifazzi.it

Proprietà letteraria riservata
Printed in Italy

Translated by Sonia Dini

ISBN 88-7246-094-8

These recipes have been collected from the live voice of countrywomen living in the surroundings of Lucca. All the indicated
quantities are meant for 4 persons. As many ingredients are typi-
cal of the region, here are some hints for the interpretation of
the recipes: the 1 day old bread often mentioned is the home
made kind, still eaten in Lucca; it lasts several days before be-
coming dry; it is used in soups when it is 1 day old because it
has a good consistency that enables it to absorb the broths
without dissolving. Any kind of home-made or country-type
bread can be used. When we say «oil», we always mean «extra-
vergin olive oil» which is produced in great quantities in the coun-
tryside of Lucca; and when we mention «peeled tomatoes», it
is for semplification but the Lucchesian countrywomen prefer
to use fresh and ripe tomatoes or, out of season, the tomatoes
they have preserved in various ways.

PASTA FRITTA

Ingredients

250g white flour (9 oz.), a little dry active yeast (approx half teaspoon), luke warm water, 1 table spoon butter, oil for frying, pinch of salt

Method

- Mix thoroughly the flour, yeast and salt, rub in the butter and slowly stir in enough lukewarm water until the mixture is the same consistency as bread dough.
- Knead the dough for a few minutes, then cover with a tea towel and leave to stand for 30- 60 mins., depending on room temperature.
- Turn the risen dough out on to a floured surface and knead again as before, cover and leave to stand for a further 30-45mins.
- Again turn the dough out onto a floured surface and roll out into a sheet about 1 cm.(approx. 1/2 inch) thick, cut the dough into preferred shapes (square, oblong, rectangular etc.) then cover them with a teatowel.
- Heat the oil in a pan until very hot (try testing it with a piece of bread first) then put the dough shapes into the hot oil a few at a time and cook for approx. 4-6mins. turning them halfway through or until golden brown.

CROSTINI DI POLLO

Ingredients

Chopped parsley, 1 onion (chopped), 1 stick celery, 1 carrot, salt and pepper, 50g. (2 oz.) chicken livers, 50g. (2 oz.) veal liver, 1/2 glass white wine, 1 tablespoon tomato puree, 2 tablespoon capers, 1 anchovy fillet bread for toasting, a little oil for frying

Method

- Heat a little oil in a pan and lightly fry the onion to a light brown.
- Add parsley, celery, carrot, salt and pepper and fry for a few mins., then add the chicken and veal livers frying for a further few minutes.
- Add the wine and the tomato puree, cover and cook over a low heat for about 30 mins.
- When cooked, remove the livers, add the capers and anchovy fillet and finely grind them together, then add the remaining ingredients and thoroughly blend all together.
- Serve the blended mixture on hot toasted bread.

PANZANELLA

Ingredients

A few slices of 1 day old bread (8-10 slices), chopped, ripe tomatoes, 1 cucumber(optional) thinly sliced, 1 medium onion thinly sliced, olive oil, 4 or 5 basil leaves finely chopped, salt and pepper

Method

Soak the bread in water, squeeze out the excess and then place in a large salad bowl.
- Add the chopped tomatoes, cucumber(if required), onion and chopped basil.
Season with olive oil, salt and pepper then mix thoroughly.
- Leave to stand for about 1 hour. Serve chilled.

PANCOTTO N. 1

Ingredients
500g. (18 oz.) chopped ripe tomatoes (peeled and seeded), finely chopped basil, salt and pepper, 1 litre (2 pints) stock, 300g (10 oz.) chopped bread crusts, 1 beaten egg (optional)

Method
- Heat a little oil in a large saucepan, add the chopped tomatoes and cook for about 5 mins.
- Add the stock, chopped basil, salt and pepper and bread crusts, bring to the boil then simmer for about 15 mins.
- Before serving, if required, beat in the egg very quickly.

PANCOTTO N. 2

Ingredients
8 slices of bread, 1/2 glass oil, 6-8 basil leaves chopped, 3 cloves crushed garlic, 500g. (18 oz.) strained tomato pulp, salt and pepper

Method
- Lightly toast the bread in the oven then crush into bread crumbs.
- Heat the oil in a large saucepan and lightly cook the crushed garlic and basil leaves, add the tomato pulp, salt and pepper, bring to the boil and simmer for 10 mins.
- Add the bread crumbs to the sauce, cover with hot water, bring to the boil and serve.
It is recommended to add a little uncooked olive oil to each bowl.

GARMUGIA

Ingredients

1 bunch spring onions 50g. (2 oz.) bacon (cut in thin strips), 150g. (4 oz.) ground beef, 400g. (14 oz.) thinly chopped vegetables (broad beans, peas, asparagues tips, artichokes etc.), 1 litre of stock, a little oil for frying

Method

- Heat the oil in a large saucepan, add the chopped spring onions, bacon and ground beef - cook for a few mins, stirring occasionally and add the prepared chopped vegetables.

- Mix well and cook for a further 15 mins stirring well.

- Add the stock and bring to the boil, allowing the mix to simmer for a few mins or until the vegetables are tender.

- Serve hot with toasted crutons.

PASTA E FAGIOLI

Ingredients
400g. (14 oz.) dark beans, sprig rosemary, 3 clovers garlic, 1 large onion, chopped, 1 small bunch parsley, chopped, 4 sticks celery, chopped, 200g. (7 oz.) chopped tomatoes or pulp, 250g. (8 oz.) pasta, Tagliatelli type, a little oil for frying, olive oil

Method
- Soak the kidney beans overnight in enough water to cover them completely.
- Strain them and again cover them with water adding 3 cloves of garlic and the sprig of rosemary
- Bring them to the boil and simmer for about 1 hour 30 mins, making sure that the water never comes below the level of the beans.
- When cooked set aside one soup ladle of the liquid and strain the rest.
- Meanwhile in a large casserole pot or saucepan fry the chopped onion, parsley and celery in a little oil until golden brown.
- Add the tomato pulp and let this mixture cook for a few mins. Add to this the beans liquid, simmer, mixing thoroughly and add the pasta.
- Remove from the heat when the pasta is cooked and add 1-2 tablespoons of olive oil to the finished dish.

MINESTRONE

Ingredients
1 small cabbage, thin strips, 1 onion, chopped, 1 carrot, chopped, 1 leak, chopped, 1 stick celery, chopped, 1 small bunch parsley,

chopped, 200g. (7 oz.) kidney beans (soaked overnight & strained)
50g. (2 oz.) bacon finely chopped, a few basil leaves, 1 sprig
thyme, 2-3 ripe tomatoes chopped (peeled & seeded), 1 litre stock,
200g. (7 oz.) pasta, salt and pepper, olive oil

Method

- Put a little olive oil into a large saucepan, add the
bacon and fry for 2-3 mins, add the onion and continue to fry for a further 2-3 mins.
- Add the cabbage, carrot, leak, celery, parsley, cover
with water and cook for about 15 mins.
- Add the kidney beans, chopped basil leaves, thyme,
tomatoes, salt and pepper and the stock.
- Simmer until the beans are cooked, then add the
pasta and continue cooking until the pasta is cooked.
- Before serving sprinkle a little olive oil in each soup
bowl.

MINESTRA DI CECI

Ingredients
300g. (11 oz.) chick peas, (soaked overnight), sprig of rosemary,
salt and pepper, 3 cloves of garlic, 5 peeled and seeded tomatoes, 200g. (7 oz.) pasta (tagliarini or rigatoni) (Do NOT use egg
noodles), olive oil

Method
- strain the chick peas and cover again in water,
preferably in a terracotta pot.
- Add the rosemary and some salt, bring to the boil
and then simmer for about 40 mins.
- Remove the rosemary and put the chick peas and
broth to one side.

- In another pan brown 3 cloves of garlic in a little oil then add the tomatoes and cook for about 5 mins.
- Remove the garlic and add this sauce to the chick peas and broth mixture.
- Mix thoroughly and return to the heat, add the pasta and continue cooking until the pasta is cooked.
This soup has to be thick and should be served very hot with a little olive oil added at the last moment.

FARRO N. 1

Ingredients

300g. (11 oz.) kidney beans, 250g. (9 oz.) dark wheat (soaked overnight in water), 1 medium onion chopped, 3 sticks celery chopped, 1 carrot chopped, 50g. (2 oz.) minced bacon, 1/2 glass oil, 1 stock cube. Enough water to cover, 1 pigs trotter (whit a spiced sausage filling cut in 2 lengthwise)

Method

- In a large pot, preferably terracotta, add all the ingredients bring to the boil and simmer with cover on for about 2 hours.

FARRO N. 2

Method

- All the ingredients are the same as the preceding recipe, but boil the beans and the pigs trotter (zampone) seperately then strain them.
- Add a mixture of chopped onions, celery and car-

rots which have previously been browned with the bacon, then the wheat.

- Cover with water, bring to the boil and simmer for at least 1 hour, adding a little more water if the soup becomes too thick.

ZUPPA CASALINGA

Ingredients

1 kg. (2 lb.) fresh beans or 400g. (14 oz.) dry beans, 700g. (1.5 lbs.) white or green cabbage (washed and chopped) 300g. (10 oz.) diced pumkin, 1 carrot sliced, 1 stick celery chopped, 4 medium potatoes diced, 2 tips of fresh fennel (finely chopped), some basil leaves & mixture of any herbs, 1/2 glass olive oil, 1 tablespoon tomato paste, salt and pepper, a few slices of lightly, toasted bread

Method

- Cook the beans in a large saucepan in enough water to cover them.

- When cooked strain the liquid into another large saucepan, add 2/3 of the beans setting aside the other 1/3 of beans.

- Add to the liquid and beans the following:

- White and green cabbage, pumpkin, carrot, celery, potatoes, fennel, basil leaves, the assortment of herbs (fresh if possible), olive oil, tomato paste, salt and pepper.

- Simmer slowly for at least 1.5 hours.

- Finally add the 1/3 beans, lightly toast the slices of bread and place them in a large soup tureen, sprinkle with a little olive oil then pour over the vegetable and bean broth.

- Let it stand for about 1 hour. Serve warm.

ZUPPA DI CAVOLO NERO & ZUCCA

Ingredients

200g. (7 oz.) kidney beans (soaked overnight), 50g. (2 oz.) minced bacon, 1 tablespoon olive oil, salt, 1/2 dark green cabbage (washed, cored & cut in strips), 300g. (10 oz.) yellow pumpkin, diced.

Method

- Rinse the beans and put into a large pot or saucepan, cover them with water, add the minced bacon, olive oil and salt
- Bring to the boil and simmer until the beans are

almost cooked, add the cabbage and continue simmering for a further 15mins., then add the pumpkin which will cook very quickly.

- Remove from the heat and serve with a sprinkling of olive oil.

This dish accompanies well with grilled herring.

ZUPPA DI CAVOLO NERO & FAGIOLI

Ingredients

350g. (12 oz.) kideney beans (soaked overnight and drained) 2 or 3 dark cabbage (remove stalk, cut leaves into strips), usual herbs and vegetables for soup. A few slices of toasted bread rubbed with garlic

Method

- Boil the the beans until tender adding all the usual herbs and vegetables for soup.
- When they are cooked, strain the broth into another saucepan and put the beans to one side.
- Bring the broth back to the boil and add the cabbage leaves, simmering for about 30 mins.
- Stir in the beans and bring back to the boil.

Serve on the toast

Note: It is quite common to reheat this soup with a little olive oil before serving.

ZUPPA DI CIPOLLA O DI PORRI

Ingredients

500g. (18 oz.) onions, sliced, oil for frying, 1 teaspoon butter, salt and pepper, 1 litre stock, 1 ripe tomato peeled & seeded, few slices toasted bread

Method

- In a large pot or saucepan brown the onions in the oil and butter, add salt and pepper.
- Stir in the stock and the tomato, simmer for about 30 mins.
- Meanwhile toast some bread and place in a large soup tureen.
- Pour over the soup and sprinkle with a little olive oil.
- Let it stand for 10 mins before serving.

The same soup can be made by substituting leaks (chopped in 1 cm slices) for the onions.

ZUPPA AL POMODORO

Ingredients

300g. (10 oz.) beans (soaked overnight), 600g. (20 oz.) chopped, ripe tomatoes (peeled and seeded), 1/2 glass olive oil, 50g. (2 oz.) chopped bacon, little oil, 1 clove garlic, toasted bread crumbs

Method

- Cover beans with water and soak overnight, drain cook in plenty of water with garlic clove and a little oil.
- Cook until beans are tender.
- Meanwhile cook the chopped tomatoes for about 10 mins. with the olive oil and the chopped bacon, set aside when cooked.

To serve this dish add some toasted bread crumbs to each bowl then add a ladle of the broth that the beans have been cooking in. Then add a few table spoons of tomato sauce followed by some beans on top with a sprinkling of olive oil.

ZUPPA DI FAGIOLINI VERDI

Ingredients
200g. (7 oz.) peeled tomatoes, small piece fo chilli pepper, or 1/2 teaspoon chilli powder, 500g. (17 oz.) green beans (runner), 2 cloves of garlic, little olive oil for frying, sprig chopped parsley, a few slices of toasted bread (rubbed with garlic, if liked), salt

Method
- Lightly fry the garlic in a little olive oil, add the peeled tomatoes, salt, chilli pepper or powder and cook for about 10 mins.
- Add the green beans with the water that they were cooked in.
- When the beans are well cooked, pour the soup into bowls over the toast.

FARINATA DI CAVOLO NERO

Ingredients
300g. (10 oz.) beans (soaked overnight), salt, 1 clove garlic, a few sage leaves, 1 dark cabbage (washed and cut into thin strips), 1 ripe tomato, chopped, 2 or 3 garlic cloves chopped, 100g. (4 oz.) minced bacon, 1/2 red pepper, maize flour

Method
- Drain the beans and cover with fresh water, adding the garlic clove and sage then bring to the boil and simmer until the beans are cooked.
- Fry the chopped garlic until light brown, add the minced bacon, chopped tomatoes and red pepper.
- When lightly cooked add this mixture to the bean broth and cook for 1 hour.
- Add sufficient maize flour to give the broth a porridge consistency, stirring continuously.
- Continue to cook for about 30 mins stirring occasionally so that the mixture is smooth and does not stick.
Serve very hot with a sprinkling of olive oil.
Note: This is an ideal dish to reheat with added olive oil, since reheating enhances the flavour.

POLENTA

Ingredients
2.5 litres (4.25 pints) cold water, 500g. (18 oz.) yellow cornmeal, 2 tablespoons, olive oil

Method
- Put the cold water in a large saucepan, add the cornmeal, salt and olive oil.
- Bring to the boil, stirring constantly with a wooden spoon.
- Simmer for about one hour.
To serve, pour the polenta over a tea towel sprinkled with yellow cornmeal or over a special wooden tray.

MATUFFI

The Matuffi are simply polenta with a little more liquid added.

Method

- Pour a few tablespoons in each soup bowl, add a sprinkling of parmesan cheese and any kind of tomato, meat or mushroom sauce.
- Leave the bowls in a well heated oven for a while before serving.

POLENTA DI NECCIO

Metric
1 litre (2 pints) of salted water, 500g. (18 oz.) chestnut flour

Method

- Bring the water to the boil and stir in the flour slowly ensuring that it does not go lumpy.
- Simmer for about 45 mins stirring constantly. If it becomes lumpy remove from heat and stir vigorously until lumps disappear.

SUGO DI CARNE

Ingredients
1 glass oil, 500g. (18 oz.) ground beef, 1 carrot, chopped, 2 sticks of celery, chopped, 1 onion, chopped, some basil leaves, chopped, salt and pepper, 300g. (10.5 oz.) peeled tomatoes, 1 tablespoon tomato paste, 20g. (1 oz.) dried mushrooms (soaked in warm water and chopped), 1 glass red wine

Method
- Chop the carrot, celery, onion and basil leaves into a mixture.
- In a large saucepan or preferably a large terracotta pot, heat the oil and add the ground beef, vegetable mixture, salt and pepper.
- Cook for about 15 mins then add the red wine, the peeled tomatoes, tomato paste and the mushrooms, including the water that they were soaking in, making sure that there is no sediment in the liquid
- Simmer over a low heat for about 1 hour.
- If the sauce becomes too thick add a few tablespoons of stock from time to time.

SPAGHETTI COL SUGO DI CARNE

Method
- Cook the spaghetti in the usual way. The Italian way is «al dente» which means very slightly underdone.
- When cooked, drain and serve with the above sauce.

SPAGHETTI ALLA PUTTANESCA

Ingredients
400g. (14 oz.) cooked spaghetti (well drained), 100g. (3.5 oz.) bologna sausage, minced, small piece chili pepper, some basil leaves, chopped, 3 cloves garlic, crushed, a little oil, 250g. (9 oz.) tomato puree (diluted with a little stock), salt and pepper

Method
- Heat the oil in a pan, add the garlic and lightly brown.
- Add the chili pepper, basil, sausage, salt and pepper, fry for a few minutes then add the tomato puree.
- Continue to cook for a further 4-5 mins then add the cooked spaghetti.
- Stir carefully and serve.

TAGLIATELLE PROFUMATE

Ingredients
400g. (14 oz.) tagliatelle (cooked «al dente»), 4 tablespoons olive oil, salt, various vegetables and herbs

Method
- Heat 4 tablespoons of olive oil in a saucepan, add some vegetables and herbs of your choice (perhaps minced garlic, rosemary and sage) brown them lightly and add salt to taste.
- Cook the tagliatelle «al dente» and drain well, then add the sauce.

TAGLIATELLE AL FUNGO CRUDO

Ingredients
400g. (14 oz.) egg noodles (tagliatelle), 50g. (2 oz.) salted butter, 100g. (4 oz.) raw pore mushrooms (must be hard, well cleaned and finely chopped)

Method
- Cook the noodles «al dente», drain well, add a little butter and the mushrooms.
- Toss thoroughly before serving.
Note: «al dente» means cooked very slightly underdone.

PAPPARDELLE CON LA LEPRE

Ingredients
400g. (14 oz.) Pappardelle pasta (shaped as a ribbon with rippled edge), 250g. (9 oz.) ground hare or rabbit meat, 1 large onion, 1 stick celery, chopped, 50g. (2 oz.) chopped bacon, 3 tablespoons olive oil, 1 glass dry white wine, salt and pepper.

Method
- Heat the oil in a large saucepan, add the onion, celery and bacon. Fry until the onion is golden brown.
- Add the rabbit or hare meat and fry for a further 5 mins or so.
- Add the white wine, simmer over a low heat for 30-45 mins stirring regularly.
- If the sauce becomes too thick add a few tablespoons of stock.
- Boil the pasta until cooked «al dente» and drain well.
Add the sauce to the papardelle and serve.

RISOTTO COI PICCIONI
O CON LE QUAGLIE

Ingredients
2 pigeons, cleaned, plus giblets, rosemary and sage, 300g. (10.5 oz.) rice, 3-4 tablespoons olive oil, salt and pepper

Method
- Heat the oil in a saucepan, add the pigeons which have been stuffed with some rosemary, sage, salt and pepper.
- Brown them, turning often for about 20 mins.
- Wash and chop giblets, add to the saucepan with a few chopped sage leaves.
- Cover and simmer for at least 1 hour.
- Remove the pigeons from the pan, bone them and return the meat to the pan.

-- Add the rice and stir in some stock little by little until the rice is well cooked.
Note: Quails can be substituted for pigeons.

RISOTTO CON FUNGHI

Ingredients
250g. (9 oz.) pore mushrooms (thoroughly washed and dried), 1 large onion finely chopped, 2 tablespoons olive oil, 300g. (10.5 oz.) rice, hot stock, salt and pepper, parsley, finely chopped

Method
- Heat the oil in a pan, chop mushrooms and add some salt and pepper.
- Cook for about 10-15 mins.
- Heat some more oil in another saucepan and add the chopped onion.
- Cook until lightly brown then add the rice.
- Stir in the hot stock little by little until rice is cooked.
- Before serving stir in the mushrooms and sprinkle with the chopped parsley.

TORDELLI

In the region of Lucca, tortelli are called tordelli
For the filling:
Ingredients
300g. (10.5 oz.) of finely ground cooked meat (50% beef and 50% pork), 1 slice of bread soaked in stock, 2 tablespons of parmesan cheese, 1 tablespoon of ground sheepsmilk cheese, 2

eggs, leaves of thyme, parsley sprig, chopped, salt and pepper

Mix all the ingredients together until well mixed, then put to one side

Method - For the pasta

- Put a largish quantity of plain strong flour on to work surface.
- Make well in the centre of the flour, add 4 eggs and a good pinch of salt.
- Work the mixture thoroughly with your hands and roll it out in very long strips (make several of these as you need one for the top and one for the bottom).
- Lay one strip out and place small spoonfuls of filling about 2 inches apart.
- Cover with another strip of the dough and close each tortello, cutting it into a half moon shape with a glass or a special cutter.
- Place them on a clean table cloth which has been dusted with white flour.
- Cook the tortelli in a large amount of boiling, salted water and cook for about 10-15 mins.
- Drain them well.
- Season them in layers in a soup tureen with a meat sauce and sprinkled with parmesan cheese.

TORDELLI SEMPLIFICATI

Method

- Using the same filling as the previous recipe, with addition of 1 egg, you can make tortelli with pasta shells from the supermarket, as this pasta shape is sufficient.

- To fill one empty shell, press another over it so any excess filling drops out from the edges.
- Cook them in the same way as the previous recipe.
- Both kinds of tortelli can be seasoned more simply with butter and some lightly browned sage leaves.

TIMBALLO DI PENNE AL SUGO

Ingredients
450g. (16 oz.) shortcrust pastry, 200g. (7 oz.) pasta cooked «al dente», 450g. (16 oz.) cold meat sauce, 1/4 (1/2 pints) litre bechamel sauce, 1 beaten egg

Method
- Line a deep 9 inch pie dish with pastry and fill with some cold «al dente» cooked pasta (penne).
- Season with a good quantity of cold meat sauce, a layer of bechamel sauce and good sprinkling of parmesan cheese.
- Cover with a thin layer of pastry, seal the edges and brush with a beaten egg.
- Cook in a preheated oven 200c for 30mins.

GNOCCHI DI PATATE

Ingredients
1 kg. (2 lb.) potatoes, 250g. (9 oz.) white plain flour, 2 egg yolks, 1 teaspoon salt, a good quantity of meat or tomato sauce, parmesan cheese

Method
- Boil and drain the potatoes, then mix them with the flour, salt and egg yolks.
- Knead the mixture thoroughly and roll into sausage shape then cut each gnocchi about 1.5 inches long.
- Boil them for about 2 mins in a large saucepan of boiling, salted water.
- Drain them a few at a time (otherwise they may break up) then layer them in a soup tureen with the meat or tomato sauce and parmesan cheese.

POLENTA CON MAIALE E SALSICCE

Ingredients
6 individual pork ribs, 200g. (7 oz.) sausages, whole or in half, 1 large onion, chopped, 50g. (2 oz.) bacon, chopped, 2 cloves of garlic, 1 sprig rosemary, finely chopped, 2-3 tablespoons olive oil, 1 glass dry, white wine, tomato sauce

Method
- Heat oil in a saucepan, lightly brown the onion, bacon, garlic and rosemary.
- Add the pork ribs fry for about 10 mins then add the wine and some tomato sauce.
- Cover and simmer for about 20 mins over a very low heat.
- Add the sausages and simmer for a further 30-40 mins over a medium heat, stirring occasionally.
- This dish must remain quite juicy in order to soak the polenta.
Serve the pork and polenta dish together.

POLENTA CON AGNELLO

Ingredients
600g. (1.5 lb.) chopped lamb, 1 large onion, chopped, 1 stick celery, chopped, 50g. (2 oz.) bacon, chopped, 1 clove garlic, crushed, a few sage leaves, finely chopped, sprig rosemary, finely chopped, 250g. (9 oz.) peeled tomatoes, 1/8 litre (1/4 pint) stock, salt and pepper, 2-3 tablesoons olive oil

Method
- Heat the oil in a saucepan, lightly brown the onion, garlic, bacon, celery and herbs.
- Add the lamb, salt and pepper and cook for about 1 hour, stirring occasionally.
- Stir in the peeled tomatoes and stock, bring to the boil and cook for a further 10-15 mins.
- This dish must remain quite moist.
Serve with the polenta.

INVOLTINI IN UMIDO

Ingredients
600g. (1.5 lb.) veal escalopes (pounded thin), 250g. (9 oz.) raw ham, a few sage leaves, 1 large onion, minced, 1 stick celery, 2-3 carrots, minced, 300g. (10.5 oz.) ripe tomatoes, chopped, 1 glass dry, white wine salt and pepper, 2-3 tablespoons olive oil

Method
- Lay the veal escalopes on a board and lay on top a slice of ham and a sage leaf.
- Roll them up and secure each one with a cocktail stick.
- Heat the oil in a saucepan, add the onion, celery,

carrot, salt and pepper and lightly brown them.
- Add the veal rolls and brown them on all sides
- Add the wine and continue cooking until the wine evaporates.
- Stir in the tomatoes and cook for a further 30-40 mins.
- If the sauce thickens too much add a little stock.

STOCCAFISSO

Ingredients
800g. (1.75 lb.) of dried cod, 400g. (14 oz.) peeled tomatoes, chopped, 1 large onion, chopped, 3 cloves garlic, crushed, 1 stick celery, chopped, basil and parsely, finely chopped, 3-4 tablespoons olive oil

Method
- Soak the cod overnight in water, drain well and cut into slices.

- Fry in half of the oil with half of the garlic and put to one side.
- Make the tomato sauce by heating the remaining oil in a saucepan.
- Add the onion, remaining garlic, celery, parsley and basil, lightly brown and add the tomatoes.
- Cook for a few mins and add the fried cod to the tomato sauce cover and simmer over a very low heat for about 2 hours, stirring occasionally.

BACCALÀ CON LA BIETOLA

Ingredients

700g. (1.5 lb.) salted cod, chopped (soaked overnight & drained), 700g. (1.5 lb.) shredded beetroot leaves, 1 large onion, chopped, 2-3 carrots, minced, 2-3 cloves garlic, crushed, 1 stick celery, chopped, basil & parsley, finely chopped, 4-5 tablespoons olive oil

Method

- Heat the oil in a very large, deep saucepan
- Add the onion, garlic, carrots, celery, parsely and basil, fry for few minutes and add the beetroot leaves.
- Brown well with the rest of the mixture and finally add the cod.
- Simmer uncovered over a medium heat for about 20 mins, carefully turning them from time to time with a wooden spoon.
- Continue cooking until the water from the beetroot leaves has been absorbed.

BACCALÀ CON I PORRI

This dish is made in the same way as the preceding recipe by just substituting the beetroot with 400g.(14oz.) of sliced leeks. If it should thicken too much while cooking just add a few tablespoons of stock.

AGNELLO AL FORNO

Ingredients
1 kg. (2 lb.) lamb in one piece, 2 cloves of garlic, sliced, a few small sprigs rosemary, 3 slices bacon cut in half, 1/2 glass olive oil, salt and pepper

Method
- With a sharp knife make about 6 holes into the piece of lamb.
- Push into the holes a sprig of rosemary, a piece of bacon, a slice of garlic, salt and pepper.
- Season the rest of the lamb with salt and pepper and place on a roasting dish with the oil.
- Cook in a preheated oven at 180C for about 1 hour, basting it from time to time with the juices.

ARISTA AL FORNO

Prepare 1Kg. (2 lb.) chine of pork in the same way as the preceding recipe, but omitting the bacon. Cook in the same way, but for better results the pork can be spit roasted.

SPIEDINI DI TORDI

Ingredients

8 cleaned and washed thrushes (stuffed with a sage leaf, salt and pepper), 1/2 kg. (1 lb.) cube pork meat, cubes of toasted bread, sage leaves, olive oil, large skewers

Method

- To spit roast or barbecue, place the thrushes on the skewers, alternating them with the bread, pork and sage leaves.
- Brush well with the oil and cook until well done.
- To cook in the oven, put all the ingredients on the skewers as before.
- Arrange them on a roasting tin and brush well with oil.
- Cook in preheated oven 180C, turning them often and basting them with their juices.
- Cook until well done.

CONIGLIO IN FORNO

Ingredients

1 kg. (2 lb.) rabbit, chopped (well washed and dried), 1 clove of garlic, 1 sprig rosemary, 1/2 glass olive oil, salt and pepper

Method

- Place the rabbit in roasting tin with the oil, garlic, rosemary, salt and pepper.
- Cook in a preheated oven 180C for about 40 mins turning often.

CONIGLIO ALLA CACCIATORA

Ingredients

1 kg. (2 lb.) rabbit, chopped (well washed and dried), 2 cloves garlic, 1 sprig rosemary, 1/2 glass olive oil, 1/2 glass dry, white wine, 400g. (14 oz.) peeled tomatoes, 150g. (5 oz.) black olives, salt and pepper

Method

- Place the rabbit in a large saucepan with the oil, garlic, rosemary, salt and pepper and fry until well browned.
- Pour over the wine and let it evaporate, turning frequently.
- Add the tomatoes and black olives and simmer over a low heat for about 40 mins.

CONIGLIO FRITTO

Ingredients

1Kg. (2 lb.) rabbit pieces (well washed and dried), seasoned flour, 2 beaten eggs, oil for frying

For the marinade:
1 glass white wine, 1/2 glass olive oil, fresh chopped parsley, salt and pepper

Method

- Heat the oil in large deep saucepan.
- Dip the rabbit pieces a few at a time in the seasoned flour and then in the beaten egg.
- Fry a few at a time until golden brown.

- Sprinkle with salt and serve.
If you wish you can marinate the rabbit pieces for a few hours or overnight. Make sure that you drain it well and pat dry before dipping it in the flour and the beaten egg. Fry as before.

POLLO FRITTO

Prepare and fry the chicken in the same way as the previous recipe. If using a marinade use the following:

1/2 glass olive oil, juice of a lemon, chopped parsley, salt and pepper.

POLLO ALLA CACCIATORA

Ingredients
1 kg. (2 lb.) chicken cut in 12 pieces, 100g. (4 oz.) bacon, minced, 1 sliced onion, 200g. (7 oz.) peeled tomatoes, chopped, 2-3 tablespoons olive oil, 1/2 glass white wine, salt and pepper

Method
- Heat the oil in a large saucepan
- Add the onion, bacon, lightly brown, then add the chicken pieces.
- Continue to brown, turning them frequently, then pour over the wine.
- Let this evaporate while still turning.
- Finally add the tomatoes, salt and pepper.
- Cover and simmer for about 40 mins stirring occasionally.
- If the sauce thickens while cooking add a little stock.

POLLO ALLE OLIVE

Ingredients

1Kg. (2 lb.) chicken in 12 pieces, 1 large onion, chopped, 2 carrots, chopped, 1 stick celery, chopped, 100g. (4 oz.) stoned, green olives, 1/2 glass white wine, 1/2 litre hot stock, 3-4 tablespoons olive oil, salt and pepper

Method

- Heat the oil in large Saucepan, add the onion, carrot, celery and lightly brown.
- Add the chicken pieces and continue frying until the chicken is also lightly brown.
- Pour over the wine and let it evaporate, stirring frequently.
- When the wine has been absorbed, add the olives, stock and seasoning.
- Simmer over a low heat for about 40 mins, stirring occasionally.

You can use the same recipe substituting rabbit for the chicken, with or without the olives.

SPEZZATINO

Ingredients

800g. (1.75 lb.) beef, pork or veal, chopped, 400g. (14 oz.) peeled tomatoes, chopped, 1 glass red wine, 2 cloves garlic, crushed, rosemary leaves, chopped, salt and pepper, 2-3 tablespoons olive oil

Method
- Heat the oil in a large saucepan and lightly brown the garlic and rosemary.
- Add the meat and cook for a further 15mins.
- Pour over the wine and when it has evaporated stir in the tomatoes, salt and pepper.
- Cover and simmer over a medium heat for about 30-40mins.
- If the mixture becomes too thick add a few tablespoons of water.

ROSTICCIANA CON OLIVE

Substitute cut pork ribs instead of meat from the preceding recipe. Cook in the same way adding 150g (5oz.) of black olives which can be fresh if preferred.

TRIPPA

Ingredients
1kg (2 lb.) of tripe, 1 onion, minced, 1 stick celery, minced, 750g. (1.5 lb.) carrots, sliced, 1 small piece chilli pepper, 1/2 glass olive oil

Method
- Wash and dry the tripe then rub on all sides with lemon.
- Cut into long, thin strips and put into a large terra cotta pot with the oil and other ingredients
- Cover and simmer over a low heat for 30 mins, stirring from time to time.

- Uncover and cook to thicken up for a further 10 mins.
- Sprinkle with parmesan cheese before serving.

UCCELLETTI CON OLIVE

Ingredients

4-5 squabs (young pigeons) per person, 1/2 glass olive oil, parsley, chopped, 2-3 cloves garlic, crushed, 1 bay leaf, 1/2 glass red wine, 150g. (5 oz.) sweetened olives

Method

- Ensure the birds are plucked and well cleaned inside and out.
- Stuff each squab with a mixture of chopped bacon, garlic, salt and pepper.
- Heat the oil in a large saucepan and add the parsely, garlic and bay leaf.
- Add the squabs, brown on all sides and pour over the red wine.
- Let it evaporate then stir in the olives and simmer for about 1 hour.

FAGIANO AL FORNO

Ingredients

1kg. (2 lb.) pheasant, 150g. (5 oz.) bacon, chopped, sage leaves, chopped, salt and pepper, 45 slices thin bacon, 3-4 tablespoons olive oil

Method

- Ensure the pheasant is plucked, cleaned and washed.

- Stuff the bird with the chopped bacon, sage leaves, salt and pepper.
- Put the stuffed pheasant in a roasting tin with the oil.
- Cover the body of the pheasant with the bacon slices and tie it up so that the bacon stays in place.
- Sprinkle with salt and pepper and cook in a pre-heated oven at 180C for about 1 hour, basting it often with the juices.

POLLO IN GRATELLA

Ingredients
1 kg. (2 lb.) chicken, 3-4 tablespoons oil seasoned with salt and pepper, juice of a lemon

Method
- Split the chicken down the breast bone and flatten with a meat mallet
- Oil the flattened chicken well on both sides
- Cook over a hot barbecue for about 15-20 mins on

each side, making sure that it is well cooked and crispy.
- Pour over the lemon juice and serve at once.

FRICASSEA

Ingredients
700g. (1.5 lb.) lamb, chopped, 1 large onion, minced, 1 stick celery, minced, 2-3 carrots, minced, 1/4 (1/2 pint) litre stock, salt and pepper, 1 tablespoon butter, 6 egg yolks, juice of a lemon, salt

Method
- Beat together the egg yolks, juice of lemon and salt and put to one side.
- Heat the butter in a large saucepan.
- Lightly brown the onion, celery and carrots, add the stock and cook for about 10 mins.
- Add the lamb, salt and pepper, then cook for about 40 mins, stirring occasionally.
- When the meat is cooked remove it from the pan onto a serving dish.
- Add the egg mixture stirring very quickly into the remaining meat juices to obtain a rich sauce.
- Pour it over the stewed meat and serve.

FEGATELLI DI MAIALE

Ingredients
600g. (1.25 lb.) pork liver (cut into cubes). Dry crumb mixture: 200g. (7 oz.) fresh breadcrumbs, 2 teaspoons ground fennel seeds,

1 teaspoon ground bay leaves, salt and pepper, olive oil, few bay leaves

Method

This recipe is supposed to be spit roast, alternating the liver and bay leaves on a spit. Another suggestion is to roll each cube into the dry crumb mixture then thread them on to skewers, like a kebab, alternating them with some bay leaves. Brush them with a little oil and cook them on a barbecue or under a hot grill, turning them often.

FEGATO ALLA SALVIA

Ingredients

500g. (18 oz.) veal liver, 1 clove garlic, crushed, ground sage leaves, white flour, juice of a lemon, salt and pepper, oil for frying

Method
- Heat the oil in a saucepan, add the garlic, sage and lightly brown.
- Add the veal liver which has been dredged with the flour.
- Cook over a high heat for 2-3 mins on each side.
- When cooked sprinkle with salt, pepper and lemon juice.
- Serve very hot.

POLLO RIPIENO

Ingredients
2kg (4 lb.) chicken small piece of beef, stock veg: carrot, onion, celery and parsely

For the stuffing:
200g. (9 oz.) ground veal, 100g. (3 oz.) ground bologna sausage, 3 eggs, 1 sliced bread soaked in milk, the excess squeezed, 1 tuft parsley 100-150g. (3-4 oz.) parmesan cheese, salt and pepper. Mix all the stuffing ingredients together

Method
- Fill the chicken with stuffing, also stuff the neck cavity.
- Place in a large pan with the giblets, beef, stock vegetables and pepper to taste.
- Simmer over a low heat for about 1.5 hours or until well cooked.
- Let cool then take the filling out of the chicken, slice it and cut the chicken into pieces and serve.

POLPETTE

Ingredients
1/2kg (1 lb.) cooked, minced meat, 1 slice bread soaked in milk and squeezed, 1 sprig wild thyme, finely chopped, 1 sprig rosemary, finely ground, 1 garlic clove, crushed, 2 eggs, salt and pepper, oil for frying

Method
- Thoroughly mix together the meat, bread, herbs, garlic, egg, salt and pepper.
- Shape into small balls, about the size of a walnut.
- Heat the oil and fry the balls a few at a time until golden brown.

POLPETTONE

The ingredients are the same as the previous recipe but instead of shaping it into small balls, shape it into a loaf shape
- Then truss it and put it into a large saucepan with some salted water and all the usual stock vegetables (carrot, onion, celery, parsely etc.)
Cook over a low heat for about 1 hour.

FRITTATA CON LE CICCHE

Ingredients
100g. (3.5 oz.) diced bacon, 5 eggs well beaten, olive oil, salt and pepper

Method
- Heat a little oil in a frying pan

- Add the bacon and cook until brown
- Pour over the eggs, add salt and pepper and cook until firm on both sides

FRITTATA CON CIPOLLE

Ingredients
1Kg (2 lb.) onions, sliced 6 well beaten eggs, 1 teaspoon salt, 2-3 tablespoons oil for frying

Method
- Heat some oil in a frying pan (the non stick sort if possible)
- Add the onions, cook with the lid on for the first 15 mins then remove it and cook until brown and the water is evaporated, stirring frequently.
- Beat the salt into the eggs and whilst stirring quickly with a wooden spoon, pour the eggs over the onions.
- Shake the pan while cooking to prevent the frittata from sticking.
- Cook well then turn upside down on to a plate and return the undercooked side to the fryingpan.
- Cook until golden brown on both sides.

FAGIOLI COTTI NEL FIASCO

For this recipe you will need an empty wine flask without the straw cover

Ingredients

1Kg (2 lb.) fresh cannelli beans, 1/2 glass olive oil, a few fresh sage leaves, 2 cloves garlic, salt, pepper and oil for serving

Method

- Put the beans into the flask.
- Add the sage, garlic and oil then completely cover with water.
- Place the flask on to a 'flameguard' over a very low heat and simmer for about 3 hours (the contents must never reach boiling point).
- When cooked drain and toss in oil with some salt and pepper.

FAGIOLI ALL'UCCELLETTO

Ingredients
1Kg (2 lb.) fresh beans cooked as before (see Pasta and Fagioli), 300g. (10.5 oz.) peeled, seeded and chopped tomatoes, 2 cloves garlic, crushed, a few sage leaves, chopped salt and pepper, 2-3 tablespoons olive oil

Method
- Heat the oil in a saucepan lightly brown the garlic and sage.
- Add the cooked and drained beans, stirring whilst cooking for a few minutes.
- Add the tomatoes, salt and pepper and simmer for about 10 mins, stirring often, then serve.

PORRI IN UMIDO

Ingredients
10 leeks (white part only), 2-3 tablespoons olive oil, 1/2 kilo (1 lb.) of peeled, mashed tomatoes or if preferred use tomato sauce, 1/2 glass water, salt and pepper

Method
- Slice the leeks into thick rounds and put them in a saucepan with the rest of the ingredients.
- Simmer over a low heat until the juice is absorbed, gently stirring occasionally and turning the leeks.

PEPERONATA

Ingredients
1 large sliced onion, 4 yellow and green peppers, 4-5 chopped

not too ripe tomatoes, 3-4 sliced potatoes, 4 tablespoons olive oil, 1/4 litre (1/2 pint) water

Method
- Put all the ingredients into a large saucepan and simmer for about 30 mins or until the potatoes are soft.
- Stir frequently

LA FRISSOGLIA

Ingredients
4-5 courgettes, sliced, 12 pumpkin flowers (optional), 100g. (3.5 oz.) fresh green beans, sliced, some fresh beetroot, chopped, 3-4 tomatoes, chopped, 3 small onions, cut in rings, some parsley, chopped, 3-4 tablespoons olive oil, 1 clove garlic, crushed, salt and pepper to taste

Method
- Prepare the pumpkin flowers (if using) by removing the stems and central core, then cut into thin strips.
- Heat the oil in a large saucepan, add the garlic and cook until light brown.
- Add all the other ingredients, cover and cook over a high heat stirring frequently.
- Cook for several minutes until all the vegetable juices have been absorbed.
- La Frissoglia is then ready to accompany a main dish.

FRITTATA DI CARCIOFI

Ingredients
1 large onion, finely sliced, 4 globe arichokes, finely sliced, 6 eggs, beaten, 2-3 tablespoons olive oil, salt

Method
- Heat the oil in a frying pan.
- Add the onion and artichokes then sprinkle with a little salt.
- Brown for about 10 mins, stirring frequently.
- Pour over the beaten eggs with a little more salt.
- Thoroughly mix the egg mixture to form a type of thick omelette and cook well on both sides.

FRITTATA DI PATATE

Ingredients
3-4 large potatoes, thinly sliced, 6 eggs, beaten, 3-4 tablespoons olive oil, salt and pepper

Method
- Heat the oil in a frying pan and add the sliced potatoes.
- Cook until soft, then if preferred drain the potatoes of oil.
- Pour over the beaten eggs with some salt and pepper and mix thoroughly.
- Cook well on both sides.

SFORMATI DI VERDURE

Ingredients
1kg (2 lb.) of vegetables of your choice, 1 glass bechamelle sauce, 5 egg yolks. Fresh dry breadcrumbs, salt and pepper

Method
- In a large saucepan boil the vegetables until tender.
- Strain them well then pass them through a sieve or chop them finely in a food processor.
- Add the bechamelle sauce, the egg yolks, salt and pepper to taste
- Pour the mixture into a buttered mould which has been coated with the bread crumbs.
- Cook in a preheated oven 180C for 40 mins.

SFORMATO VERDE

Ingredients
1kg (2 lb.) spinach, 300g. (10.5 lb.) ricotta cheese, 50g. (1.5 oz.) parmesan cheese, grated, 2 whole eggs, 2 egg yolks, 2 egg whites stiffly beaten fresh, dry bread crumbs

Method
- Boil the spinach and when well cooked drain well, sqeezing out all excess water.
- Chop very finely and blend in the ricotta cheese, parmesan, the whole egg and yolks, also adding salt and pepper to taste.
- Finally fold in the stiffly beaten egg whites.
- Pour the mixture into a buttered mould which has been sprinkled with the breadcrumbs.
- Cook in a preheated oven 200C for 30 mins.

SFORMATO SEMPLICE

Ingredients
1kg. (2 lb.) of boiled vegetables, drained. Dry breadcrumbs. Handful of parmesan cheese, 1 teaspoon fresh thyme, chopped. Butter, salt and pepper

Method
- Puree the vegetables then add a good handful of breadcrumbs, parmesan cheese, the thyme, salt and pepper to taste.
- Turn the mixture into a buttered roasting tin or mould which has also been sprinkled with dry breadcrumbs.
- Cover the top with breadcrumbs and dot with butter.
- Cook in a preheated oven 180C for about 40 mins.

INSALATA CAMPAGNOLA

Ingredients
1 head of lettuce, washed, 1 onion, finely chopped, 2 hard-boiled eggs, chopped

Dressing
2 fillets of anchovy, minced, 3 tablespoons olive oil, 1 tablespoon lemon juice or vinegar, salt and pepper

Method
-Place the lettuce, onion and eggs in a large salad bowl
- Beat all the ingredients for the dressing together
- Pour over the salad, toss well and serve

POMODORI RIPIENI

Ingredients
8 large tomatoes, very firm, 300g. (10 oz.) of ground, cooked beef, 1 slice bread, soaked in milk, 1 egg, grated parmesan cheese, 1 teaspoon thyme, chopped, 1 teaspoon parsley, chopped, 1 clove garlic, crushed, salt and pepper, 2-3 tablespoon olive oil

Method
- Cut the tops off of the tomatoes and scoop out the inside with a teaspoon.
- Mix all the other ingredients together except the oil.
- Stuff the tomatoes with the mixture then heat the oil in a pan.
- Place the stuffed tomatoes in the pan and simmer over a low heat, turning them over to let them cook on both sides.
- Add a little water if they start to burn.

PEPERONI RIPIENI

Follow the previous recipe but use peppers instead of the tomatoes and cook in the same way.

FOGLIE DI CAVOLO RIPIENE

Ingredients
About 10 large leaves from a white cabbage. The same stuffing as the recipe for stuffed tomatoes. Some olive oil. Tomato sauce. Salt

Method
- Boil Some water in a large saucepan and add a teaspoon of salt.
- Drop the cabbage leaves into the water and cook for a few minutes then drain them well.
- Lay each cabbage leaf out on a board, add some of the stuffing then roll up into a parcel shape.
- Secure them with a cocktail stick.
- Heat some oil in pan and cook them with some tomato sauce.

FIORI DI ZUCCA RIPIENI

Ingredients and Method
- Pick about 15 marrow or pumpkins flowers when they are wide open (these must be freshly picked).
- Cut the flowers so that you keep just a small piece of the stem and throw away the little needle-shaped leaves around the main stem.
- Fill the flowers with the same stuffing as the stuffed cabbage leaves.
- Close the flowers by folding them over the stuffing.
- Cook in the same way as the cabbage leaves.

STRINGHE IN UMIDO *

Ingredients
1kg (2 lb.) of haricot vert, cut into small pieces, 400g (14oz) tomatoes, peeled and mashed, 2 cloves of garlic, crushed, some basil leaves, 1 glass of water, salt and pepper, olive oil

Method
- Put all the ingredients into a large pan, simmer over a low heat, stirring often.
- Cook until all the juice is absorbed.
- Continue to cook for a few minutes more until the mixture is quite dry, but make sure that they do not burn.
* In Lucca haricots vert are called «strings».

ZUCCHINI IN UMIDO

Ingredients
1kg (2 lb.) courgettes, cut into thick slices, 250g (9oz) tomatoes, peeled and mashed, 2 cloves garlic, crushed, 2-3 tablespoons olive oil, some catmint leaves, salt and pepper

Method
- Put all the ingredients into a large pan, cover and simmer over a low heat for about 20 mins, stirring often, making sure not to break up the courgettes.

ZUCCHINI RIPIENI

Ingredients
12 courgettes. Filling using the same as for stuffed tomatoes

Method
- Cut the courgettes in half (lengthways) and with a teaspoon empty out the middle (so that they look like little boats).

- Fill them with the stuffing and place them in roasting pan with a little olive oil.
- Cook in a preheated oven 180C for about 40 mins.

FUNGHI IN UMIDO

Ingredients
500g (1 lb.) of young pore mushrooms, washed and thinly sliced, 3 cloves of garlic, crushed, sprig of catmint, 2-3 tablespoon olive oil, 1 tablespoon of tomatoe sauce

Method
- Heat the oil in a pot (preferably terracotta) and add the garlic and catmint.
- Add the mushrooms and cook over a low heat.
- When they are half cooked add the tomato sauce.
- Stir well and cook until nicely browned.

FUNGHI IN GRATELLA

Ingredients
Some pore mushroom caps, washed and dried, 2 cloves of garlic, crushed, catmint leaves, olive oil, salt and pepper

Method
- Place the mushrooms on to a wire rack over a baking tray.
- Sprinkle with the oil, garlic, catmint leaves, salt and pepper.
- Cook in the oven on a low heat.

NECCI

Ingredients
500g (17.5 oz.) of chestnut flour, water, 1/2 teaspoon salt, oil

Method
- Make a batter with the flour, water and salt. This batter must be a little more livid than custard.
- Heat up some waffle irons, open them and oil on both sides.
- Make the waffles with batter, making sure to cook both sides
- Serve with fresh ricotta cheese.

TULLORE

This is simply made with dry chestnuts, boiled for

about 1 hour in salted water. Serve them with their own cooking broth.

PASIMATA

This is a simple bread rectangular in shape. The two long sides have a rippled edge with aniseeds baked in. It is traditionally eaten at Lent and blessed on Easter Day.

TORTA DI NECCIO

Ingredients
500g (17.5 oz.) chestnut flour, water, 1/2 taespoon salt, 2 tablespoons olive oil, sprig rosemary, walnut kernals

Method
- Make a batter with the flour, water, salt and oil.
- Pour on to a large well oiled baking pan and sprinkle the surface with the chopped rosemary and walnut kernals plus a little extra oil.
- Cook in preheated oven at 180C for about 1 hour.

BUCCELLATO

Ingredients
Metric
500g. (18 oz.) plain flour, 150g. (5.5 oz.) sugar, 20g. (1 oz.) aniseeds, 15g. (1/2 oz.) of active dried yeast, some luke warm water, 50 raisins, 1 egg white lightly beaten

Method
- Melt the yeast with a little luke warm water and blend with a small amount of flour, set aside for while.
- Mix the yeast with the remaining flour and the rest of the ingredients, except the beaten egg white, to form a dough being the same consistency as bread dough.
- Form the dough into a ring shape and set aside to rise for a while, then place on to greased baking tray. Coat the surface with the beaten egg white and some sugar syrup.
- Cook in a preheated oven 180C for about 45mins.

ZUPPA LUCCHESE

Ingredients
Some slices of buccellato. A quantity of 'vin santo', sugar, strawberries, soaked in wine, a quantity of custard

Method
- Dip some slices of buccellato in the 'vin santo' and place them at the bottom of a large bowl or soup tureen.
- Cover them with a thin layer of sugar then a layer of strawberries and finally a layer of custard.
- Keep layering in this way until the bowl is filled finishing with a layer of custard.

LE RICETTE DI NONNA DORA

The following recipes are from the personal recipe book of Mrs. Dora Mennucci.

CAPPELLI DI PINOCCHIO PIENI IN BRODO

Ingredients
300g. (10.5 oz.) ground beef, 50g. (2 oz.) salami, minced, 2 eggs, beaten, grated parmesan cheese, handful of parsley, chopped, sprig of wild thyme, chopped, salt and pepper

Method
- Mix the ground beef with the minced salami and sit in the beaten eggs, the parmesan cheese, parsley

and wild thyme, then season with salt and pepper.
- Fill the 'cappelli di Pinocchio' with this mixture and close them.
- Cook in boiling water.

POLPETTE

Ingredients
400g. (14 oz.) ground beef, 100g. (3.5 oz.) bread, crusts removed and soaked in milk, 2-3 tablespoons white wine, 3 eggs, 1/2 teaspoon nutmeg, grated, handful parmesan cheese, grated, salt and pepper, oil for frying, 1 tablespoon tomato sauce

Method
- Heat a little oil in a saucepan and add the ground beef and white wine.
- Fry until almost done then add the tomato sauce and remove from the heat.
- Add the bread to the meat squeezing out the excess milk beforehand.
- Mix in the eggs, cheese, nutmeg, salt and pepper.
- Mix well, then form into meatballs, dredge them with flour or dry breadcrumbs and cook them in hot oil until nicely browned.

POLPETTONCINO IN SALSA

Ingredients
400g (14 oz.) ground beef, 1 small slice bread soaked in milk,

2 eggs, handful parmesan cheese, grated, 1/2 teaspoon nutmeg, salt and pepper

Ingredients for sauce
1 tablespoon butter, 4 tablespoons oil, 1 small onion, thinly cut, 4 carrots, thinly sliced, 1 stick celery, thinly chopped, stock or broth

Method
- Mix the ground beef, egg, bread, cheese, nutmeg, salt and pepper and form the mixture into a meat loaf, then coat it in dry breadcrumbs.
- Melt the butter with the oil in a large pot.
- Place the meatloaf in the pot and brown it well on all sides then remove from pot.
- Cook the onion, carrot and celery in the same pot, browning them lightly.
- Place the meat loaf back into the pot with some stock or broth and cook for about 1 hour.
- To serve, slice the meatloaf then pour over the sauce.

TORTA CO' BECCHI

Ingredients for the pie
100g. (3.5 oz.) butter, 200g. (7 oz.) sugar, 1 tablespoon oil, 1 egg, 1 level coffee spoon, baking powder, 300g. (10.5oz.) flour to make a soft dough, pinch of salt

Ingredients for the filling
100g. (3.5 oz.) bread soaked in milk, 100g. (3.5 oz.) cooked rice, 1 small boiled beetroot, finely chopped, handful of parmesan cheese, grated, 2 eggs, 50g. (2 oz.) sugar, 1/2 teaspoon cinnamon, salt and pepper

Method
- Work the dough quickly and line a 12 inch pie dish, leaving enough of the dough to make the 'Becchi' (these are little pointed cones of dough which make the pie look like a crown)
- Mix all the ingredients for the filling well and pour into the pie shell.
- Sprinkle the surface with some thin slices of butter, add a little oil and a pinch of cinnamon.
- Shape the edge of the pie and bake in a preheated oven 180C for about 50mins.

CONFETTI DELLE SPOSE

Ingredients
8 egg yolks, beaten, 100g. (3.5 oz.) aniseeds, 1kg (2.2 lb.) flour, 500g. (18 oz.) sugar, 1 glass honey, 200g. (7 oz.) melted butter, pinch of salt

Method
- Place the flour and sugar together on a board, make a well in the middle and pour in the butter, egg yolks, honey and aniseeds.
- Mix well together to form a dough, roll this and make lots of finger shapes 2-3cms (1.5 inches) long.
- Dredge a cookie sheet with yellow cornmeal and place the 'confetti' (the finger shapes) on to the cookie sheet.
- Bake in a preheated oven 200C for about 1 hour. These confetti are used in the mountains surrounding Lucca in substitution for the almond confetti which were very rare.

INDEX

finito di stampare
nel mese di agosto 1999
dalla «litografia varo», pisa
per conto di mp maria pacini fazzi editore